HOW TO BECOME YOUR SUPERHERO

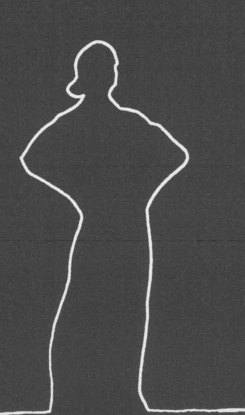

RUBEN VIGLINO

To order additional copies of this book, contact:
Xlibris
AU TFN: 1 800 844 927 (Toll Free inside Australia)
AU Local: 0283 108 187 (+61 2 8310 8187 from outside Australia)
www.xlibris.com.au
Orders@Xlibris.com.au

ISBN: Softcover   978-1-6641-0249-1
         Hardcover   978-1-6641-0250-7
         EBook   978-1-6641-0248-4

Print information available on the last page

Rev. date: 12/22/2020

I learned a lot from you.
Then when i moved away, the world taught me a lot, this writing and these thoughts of mine are what I bring back home, to you, with gratitude, for all that you have offered me.
With the certainty and reassurance that I am making the best use of the greatest gift you have given me ... life.

Thanks Mom!

Special thanks to Esther Hicks and Abraham Hicks.

Your words and teachings have helped me and led me to observe life in a way that I never thought possible.
Thank you for this new perception.
Today I can say that I live a dream.
I was looking for something magical and searched everywhere and I could not find it because I was looking for it in the wrong places.
But that secret was already part of me, the only place I hadn't looked.
All the answers have always been there, I just had to listen.

There are no words that can describe my gratitude for you, hoping that one day our paths will cross.
Thanks Esther

Ruben

Why this book?

One day I was walking on the beach, wearing my Superhero T-shirt when I met a child.
He gazed up at me, a deep look, an almost exalted expression that I will never be able to forget.
After a few moments of amazement he asked me if I was the real Superman.
I looked at him smiling, and also a little pleased, and said "yes".
The boy ran with happiness and started shouting out his amazing discovery for all to hear.
Many adults, attracted by his enthusiasm, looked at him amused and smiled for they were happy for the child, but they did not feel what he felt, for no one more than that child could have felt closer to reality.

It was that boy, with his enthusiasm and his imagination that made me a real Superhero.
That same day I decided to tell my story to all those who are still able to dream.
I decided to reveal to them the secret that led me to the creation of "my " Superhero.

The secret that can lead each of us to be a Superhero.

HOW TO BECOME YOUR SUPERHERO

Once upon a time, there was a child who had many dreams and many desires.
He was a passionate, joyful child and so eager to make all his dreams come true.
He knew that anything could be possible for him and he truly believed it.

He also knew how important it was for a child to play and how important it was to have fun and enjoy life happily.
He was very eager to learn, but did not like school and he did not study very much.

Every day he asked the grown-ups questions, but for some incomprehensible reason, the answers he received did not satisfy him.
He began to wonder why adults tried to complicate everything and why they were always so worried. They often spoke of "reality", but spoke of it in such a way as to make any change seem impossible.

He then observed that adults almost never talked about their dreams and began to wonder if growing up he would become like them.

Over the years he began to observe the grown-ups more and more carefully.

He always saw them running, very busy, but it seemed that they did not know exactly where they were going.

He saw them do many things, but without joy on their faces, and he did not understand why they continued to do what they really did not like to do.

They called it "work", but it seemed that work was not a fun thing to do.

At this point, the child wondered if, once grown up, there was no way to do what you really love.
He felt there had to be a way.
He could not understand any other way of living other than his own.

It seemed, in his eyes, that the grown-ups were interested in completing more and more tasks and always in the shortest time frame possible.
He saw them struggling and often in a bad mood.
With the passage of time, he began to believe that realizing your dreams and doing what you love in your life was not a very simple thing to do.

The most recurring topic that the grown-ups had was money and it seemed that most of their attention was on focussed on this.
The adults no longer played and he thought that perhaps as time pressed on, they had forgotten how to do it.

At the age of seven the boy looked in the mirror and observing himself carefully, he wondered what the secret of life was.
He knew well, that that secret existed and that he had only to find it, or rather, find it again.
He knew it was already somewhere inside of him and so he began his search.

After years of searching, he felt that if he really wanted to find his hidden secret, he simply had to stop looking for it.
Only in this way his secret would be revealed to him.

When that child became a boy, he began to study and work by doing things he did not like but he was told by society were the right things to do.
This seemed to be the way the adult world worked. Life no longer seemed fun to him, it was as if the magic was gone.
To make matters worse, he was also forgetting how to play.

He knew, that was not the way he wanted to live and that he could not allow the grown-ups to be right.
He also knew that, in one way or another, he would find the solution, and so he decided to listen only to those who were truly happy.

As the boy became an adult himself, he chose to move and live far away from his humble beginnings, to start all over again and follow his dreams.
He was elated by this new change and began to accept all the challenges that faced him with courage and boldness.

He wanted, now more than ever, to turn his dreams into reality, and he was willing to make many sacrifices to achieve this. He wanted to show everyone how important it was to follow their dreams so he started working harder than ever on them.

But something was still not working, and he discovered that working so hard wasn't all that fun.

It was perhaps the idea of working that he didn't like. He had become like the grown-ups, more focused on what he wanted to get done instead of feeling love for what he was doing.

That was not the way to be happy.

That's when he realized, what he was really looking for was happiness.
The simple emotion, the feeling of love for what he was doing.

Although he continued to make mistakes he knew that focusing on them would not help him, but would further magnify the problem.
He knew that the solution was already inside him somewhere, he had only to find it, simply by listening to himself.

He stopped turning back and decided he wanted to look forward and in the direction that made him happier.
He felt that love for his dreams was the right way, but for some reason he could no longer love them.
In fact, feeling the distance it would take to reach them made him sad.

Failing to find love within himself, he looked outwards and found
that he could find love whenever he felt happy.
So he went in search of happiness.
He believed this way, he could make love possible and
therefore he would have found all of the solutions.

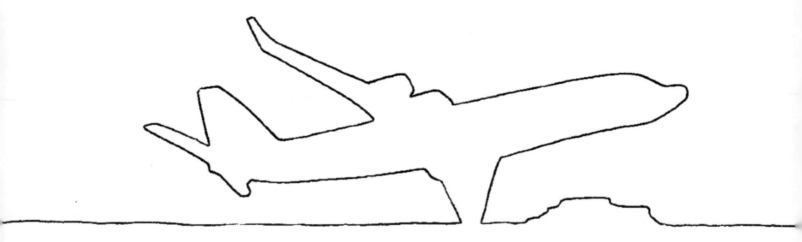

But he soon realised that he had been concentrating on this conclusion for so long that he had almost forgotten how to have fun.

One day, walking on the beach, something important came to him, something that completely changed his life.

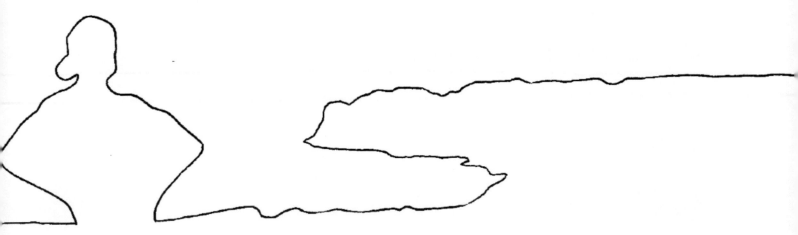

Finally, he realized that being happy depended on his degree of attention to the positive aspects, in any area and in any situation.
He also understood that people can perceive and experience the same situation in completely different ways and so he decided he wanted to see more of the positive aspects of life and to enhance all that made him feel really good.

Focusing on the positive and beautiful things in life made those same aspects bigger and more important and the negative and painful aspects almost disappeared.
However, it was sometimes difficult to find these positive aspects in certain events, facts and even people's behaviours.

Instead, what he was really looking for were the emotions that are found in the greatest aspects that this planet has to offer. He was aware now that any emotions he was looking for were at his reach, he just needed to find them in different places.

Sometimes abundance of money was hard to feel, but he knew that there was abundance in the air we breathe, in how much love there can be in a thought, an idea or a simple intention. Sometimes it can be hard to find the path to your own well-being, but he could see the well-being represented by the water that follows a stream and flows to its destination, knowing where it needs to go and that it can be this easy for us too.

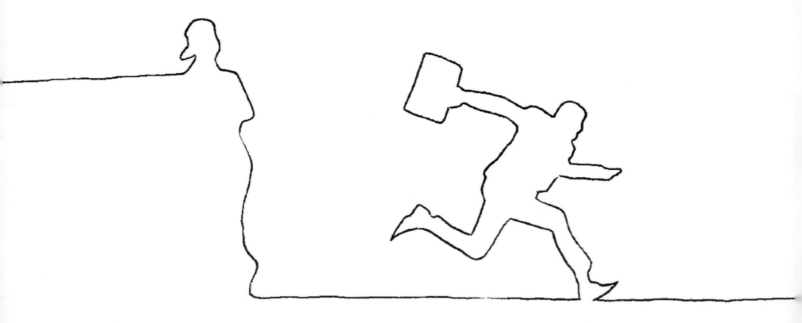

From that moment on, the boy understood that it is not essential and becomes counterproductive, to focus on what you want to change or improve.
Instead it is important to focus on your own flow.
The emotions you would like to feel, the way you would like to live and what you want to achieve.

When you know how to grasp the emotions you thought would derive from an event, fact or success, you no longer need to grasp them, for they will come on their own.

From that moment on he felt like a Superhero and he knew that for him, everything would be possible for he was now perfectly aware of the fact that life was given to us to make our dreams come true and that there is no other way to live.

So just like that child at the beginning of my story, I wanted to spread this secret and share it with everyone.
Everyone deserves to become their own Superhero and in fact, each of us already are superheroes, we have simply forgotten how to use our super powers.

Super powers that are available to us whenever we love and whenever we are happy.
They have been given to us as a gift and to find them, we must only give attention to the voice in our heart.

So here is the recipe to become your own Superhero:

Focus on everything that makes you feel good and makes you happier.
Happiness will open the doors for love, and when you love, everything you most desire in your life will take shape and be realized.

Grown-ups don't know everything and have forgotten so much, but above all, they don't clearly see what's in your heart and maybe you can't either, but you can hear it clearly.
So do what you love, do what makes you happy and if you decide not to listen to your heart, you're deciding to allow yourself to be disrupted from your intended path.

I've always liked the idea of writing and I've always felt inspired to write but at school my ideas and themes were not understood and were never good enough. But I wasn't going to let this hold me back, and I knew my voice and my themes had to be heard and here I am now, writing books.

Everything works when you believe it will.

Vizko.

"Create your own reality"

— Ruben Viglino

"Citius Altius Fortius"

— Fulvio Roattino

Printed in the United States
By Bookmasters